DRAW SUPER HEROES!

DAVID OKUM

IMPACT
CINCINNATI, OHIO
www.impact-books.com

How to Use This Book

There are three or four steps for each hero.

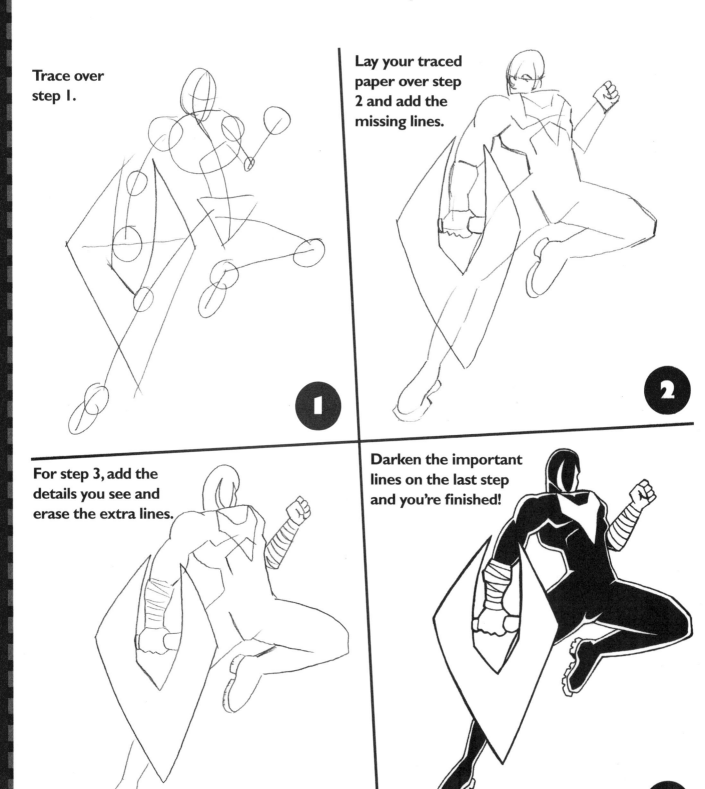

Trace over step 1.

1

Lay your traced paper over step 2 and add the missing lines.

2

For step 3, add the details you see and erase the extra lines.

3

Darken the important lines on the last step and you're finished!

4

Basic Shapes

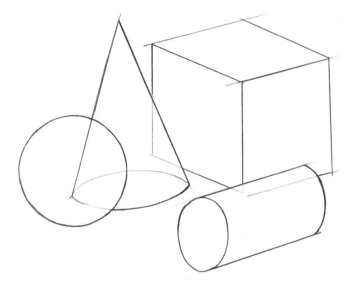

Everything is made up of basic shapes: circles, squares, rectangles and triangles. You can combine the shapes to draw almost anything.

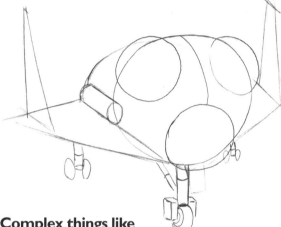

Complex things like this delta wing shuttle are basic shapes too!

Even people and heroes are just a bunch of shapes.

Noses

Noses are made up of circles, ovals and lines.

Draw nostrils as thin ovals or lines, never as pig-like circles.

The sides look like ovals.

The end of the nose looks like a circle.

Drawing Eyes

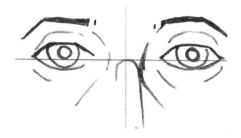

Eyes are made up of circles inside circles.

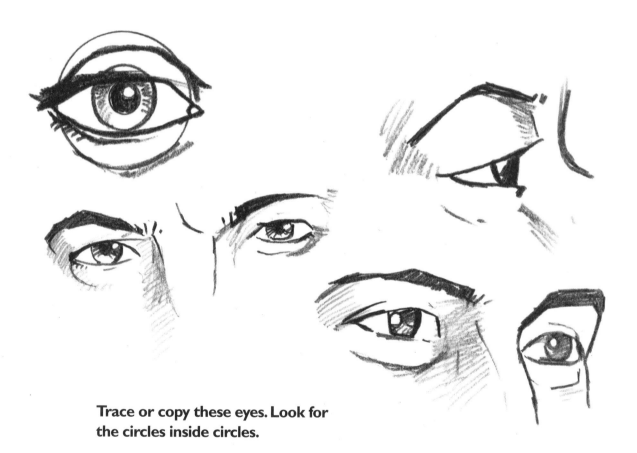

Trace or copy these eyes. Look for the circles inside circles.

Drawing Mouths

The center of the mouth is a bow shape that points down.

The upper lip is thinner than the lower lip

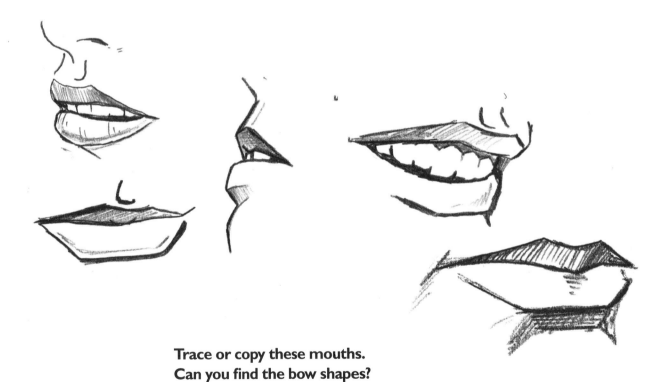

Trace or copy these mouths. Can you find the bow shapes?

Drawing Ears

**The shapes inside the ear can be hard to draw.
Just keep your lines simple.**

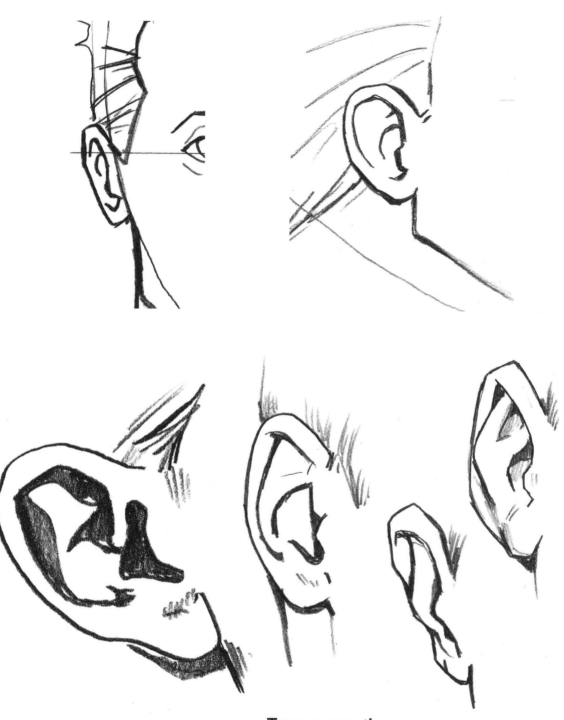

Trace or copy these ears.
Look for the shapes.

Face, Front

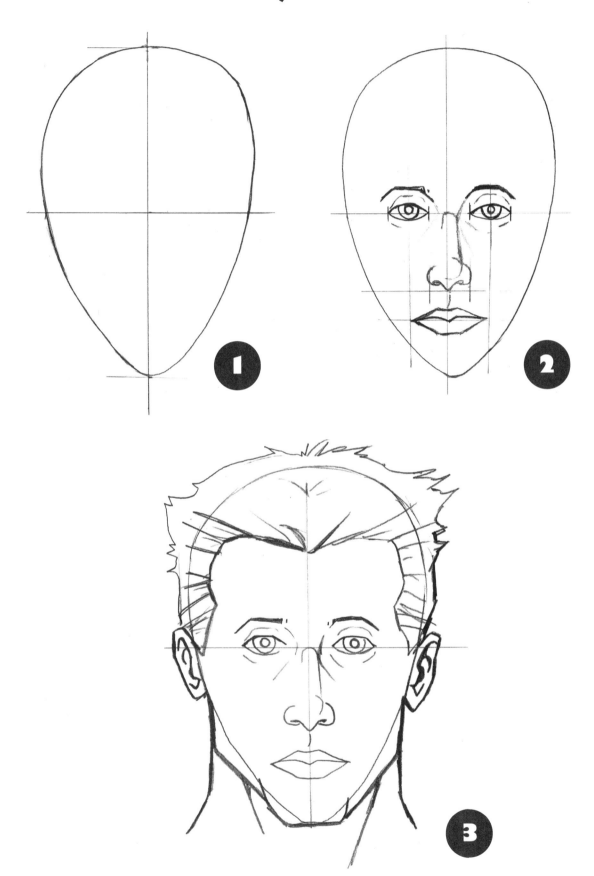

Face, Side

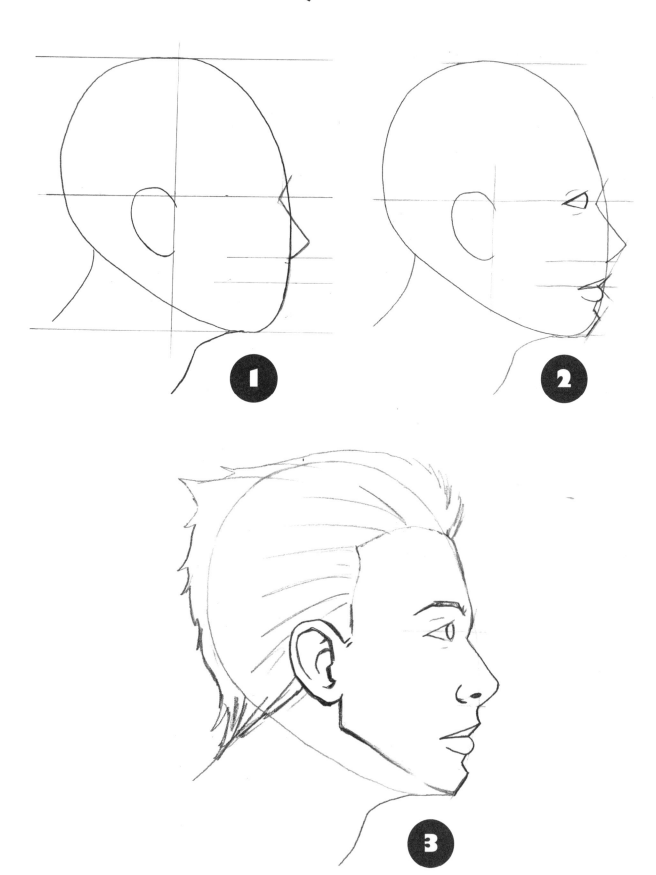

Face, 3/4 View

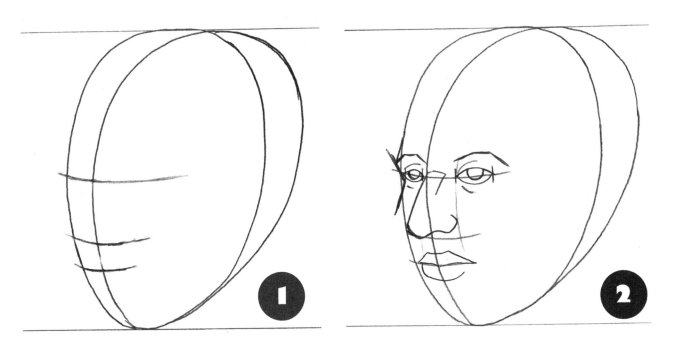

How Big is a Super Hero?

Your heroes can be as big as you want them to be. Here are a couple rules to keep them looking their best.

The regular male super hero is from 8 to 8½ heads tall. Normal males are around 7½ to 8 heads tall.

Superhuman men range from 9 to 9½ heads tall.

The neck is about ¼ of the head.

Hands are about the size of the face from chin to eyebrows.

Legs and feet take up half of the total body.

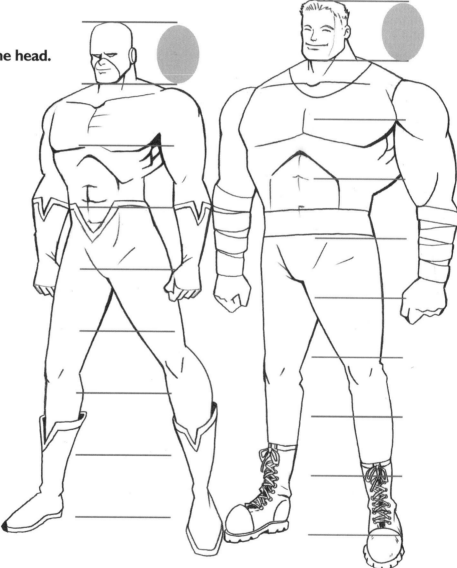

Adult Male

A regular female super
hero ranges from 8 to 8½
heads tall, while normal
females are only 7½ to 8
heads tall.

Superhuman women range
from 8½ to 9 heads tall.

**Shoulders are about
2 heads apart.**

**Waist is roughly 2
heads wide.**

**Legs and feet take up
half the total body.**

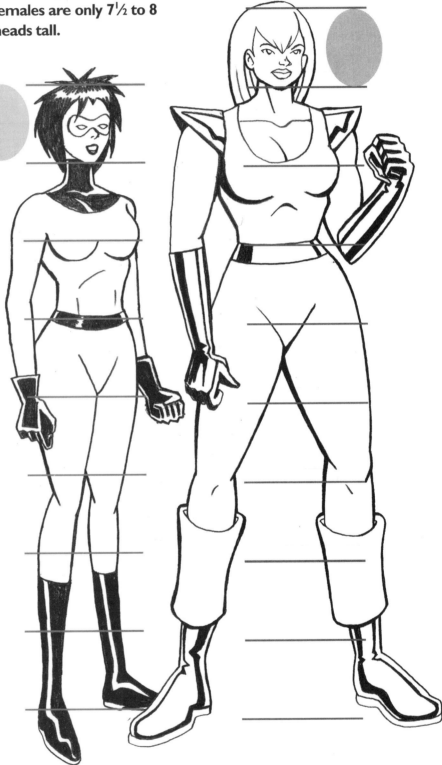

Adult Female

Teens range from 7 to 7½ heads tall

Some have rounder faces and bigger eyes

Shoulder width is 1½ to 2 heads

Wrists begin at the halfway mark.

Kids are 4½ to 5 heads tall.

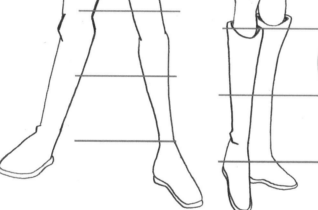

Large eyes and head

Teens

Bigger hands and feet

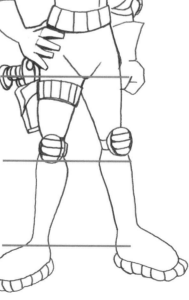

Kids

Extreme Bodies

Almost anything goes in comic books. Compare these extreme characters to the classic super hero.

Classic super hero   **Thin robot**   **Ape-bot**   **Steam-driven nightmare**

Making robots look cool is the most important thing in comics. Decide how they work after you draw them.

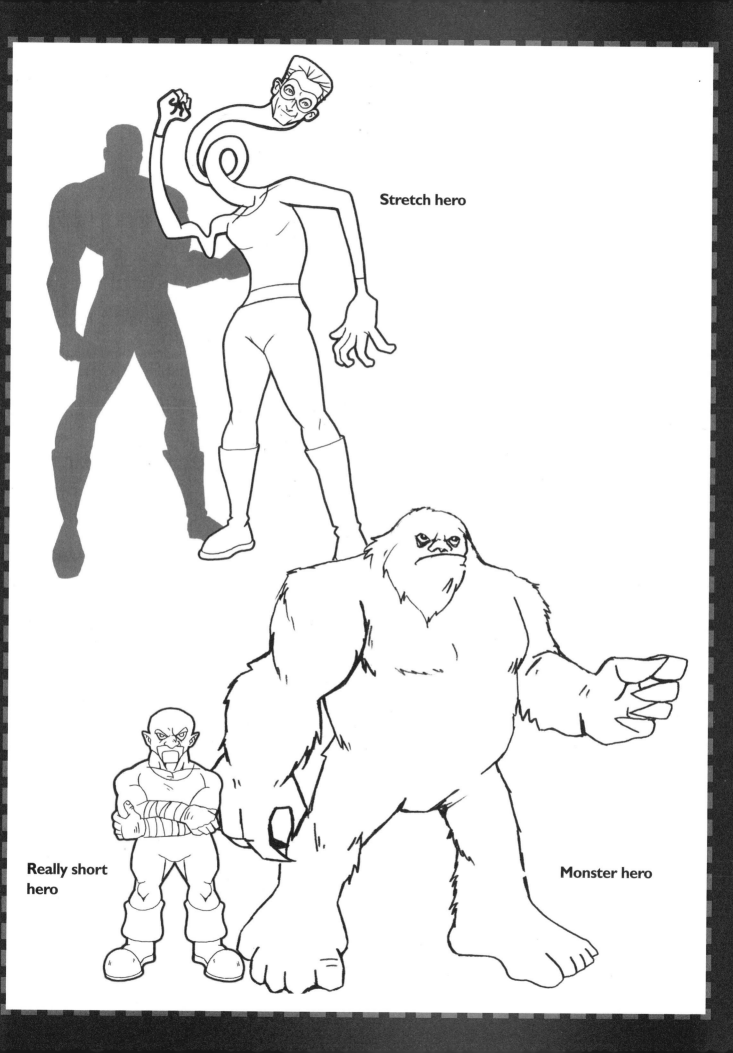

Stretch hero

Really short
hero

Monster hero

Drawing Hands

Hands start with shapes just like everything else.

Keep the thumb over the fingers to draw a fist.

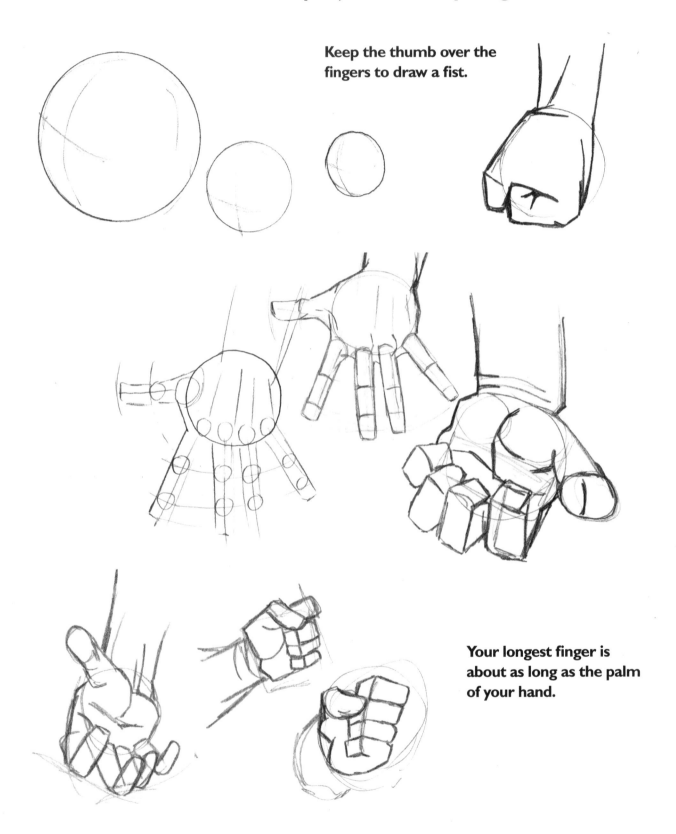

Your longest finger is about as long as the palm of your hand.

Drawing Feet

Look at the shapes in feet! Trace or copy some of the feet on this page.

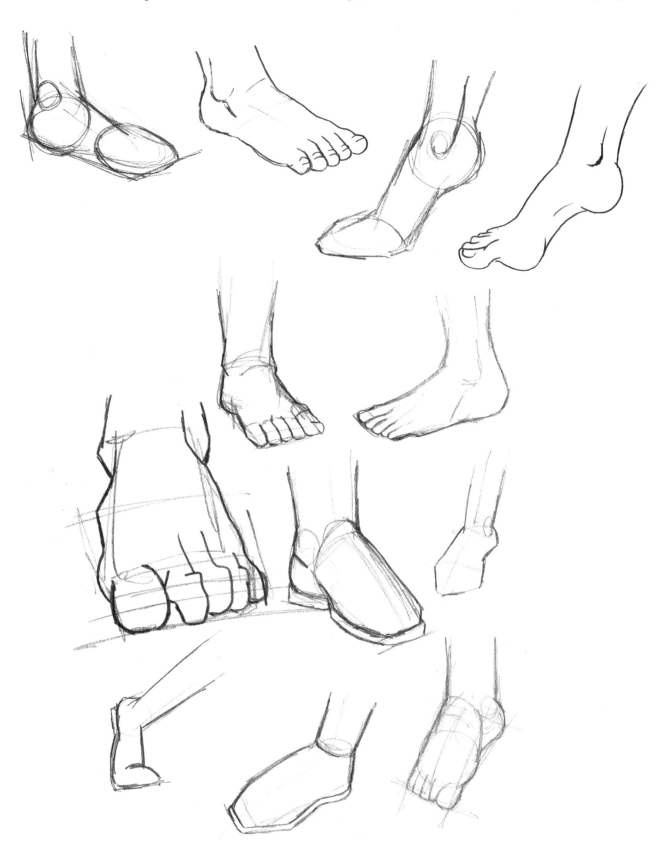

Super Powers and Effects

You can draw super powers almost any way you want. Here are some ideas to get you started. Trace or copy the powers, then make up some of your own!

Energy Blasts

Blasts can come from hands, eyes, mouths or even hair.

Glowing Hands

Circles show magic or mental power.

Fire Power

Trace or copy the flames coming from this teen hero's hands.

Bullet Holes

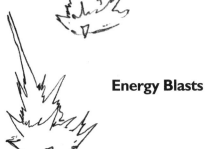

Energy Blasts

Machine-Gun Blasts

Shock Waves

Ultimate Hero

The Scarlet Avenger

ORIGIN: Cosmic rays turned this former pilot into one of Earth's strongest heroes.
POWERS: Super strength and energy bolts.

Detective Hero

Minerva

ORIGIN: One of a long line of heroes supported by a secret group that follows
Minerva, the Roman goddess of wisdom and war.

POWERS: No known superpowers but is trained to top human fighting powers.

Flying Hero

Starlighter

ORIGIN: Her powers come from the magic wand a strange wizard gave to her.
POWERS: Flight, star beam blasts and force field.

Power Armor Hero

Windburn

ORIGIN: Jessica Mathers made the Windburn armored suit for the government.
POWERS: Armored shell. Flight and blaster systems.

The Sidekick

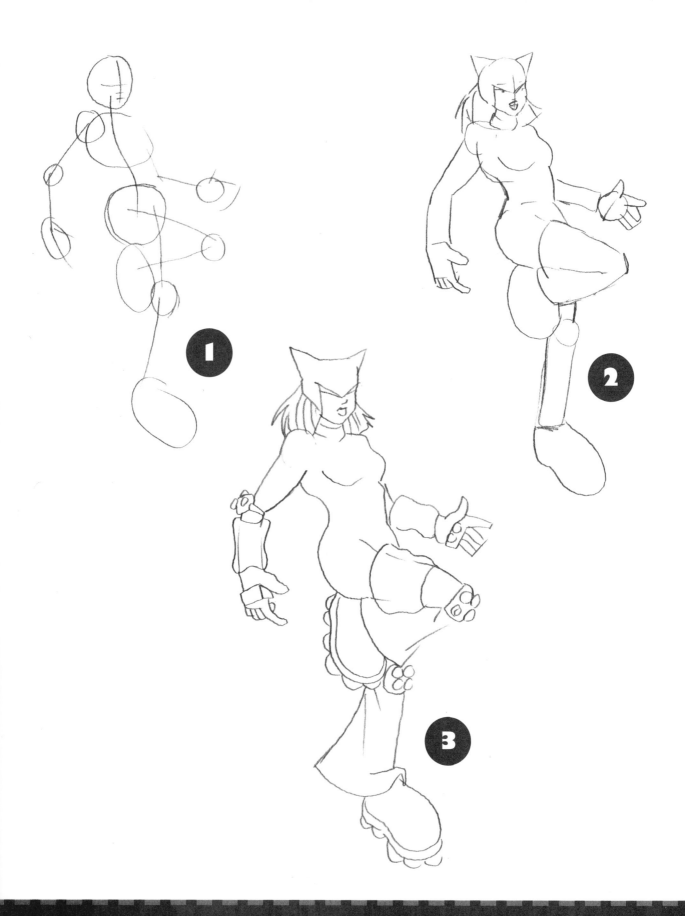

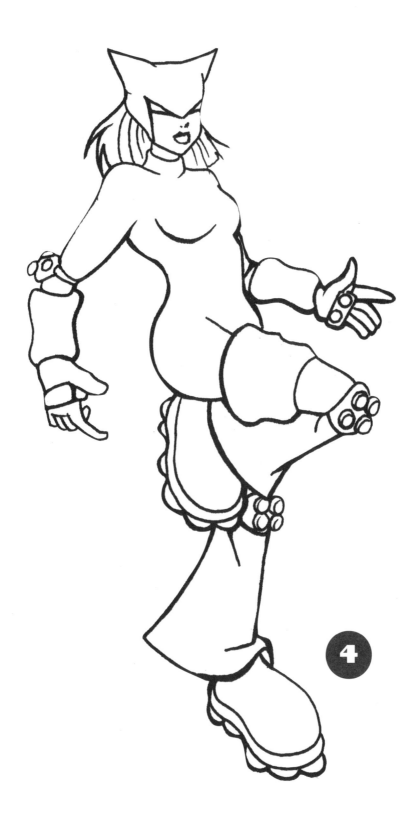

④

Gargirl

ORIGIN: Became the sidekick of the hero Kimera after he saved her parents from a fire.
POWERS: No special powers, but uses homemade gadgets like suction cups for climbing.

The Magic Master

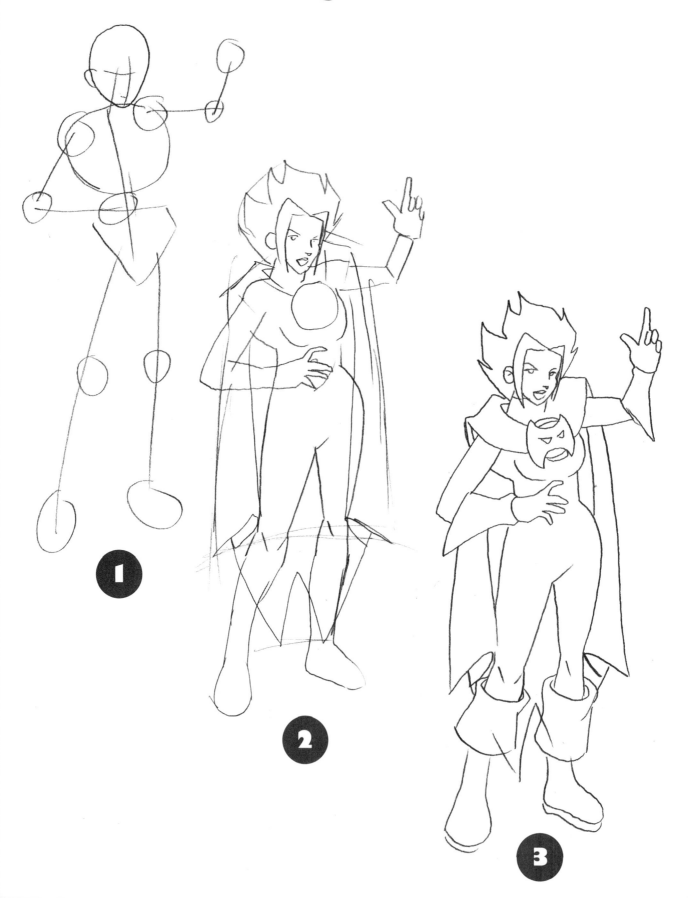

4

The Sorceress

ORIGIN: Blasted into the present from the 12th century.
Comes from a time when magic was common.
POWERS: All things magical.

Gadget Hero

Azadim

ORIGIN: After working on a top-secret war project, Azadim built a
collection of gadgets to do his own research.
POWERS: His gadgets allow him to find and catch bad guys. He has no superpowers.

Big Tough Guy

The Mighty Blue Genie

ORIGIN: Quiet shopkeeper Payne Gray found a magic lamp in his store. He turns into the Mighty Blue Genie every time he rubs the lamp.
POWERS: Superstrong.

Fantasy Hero

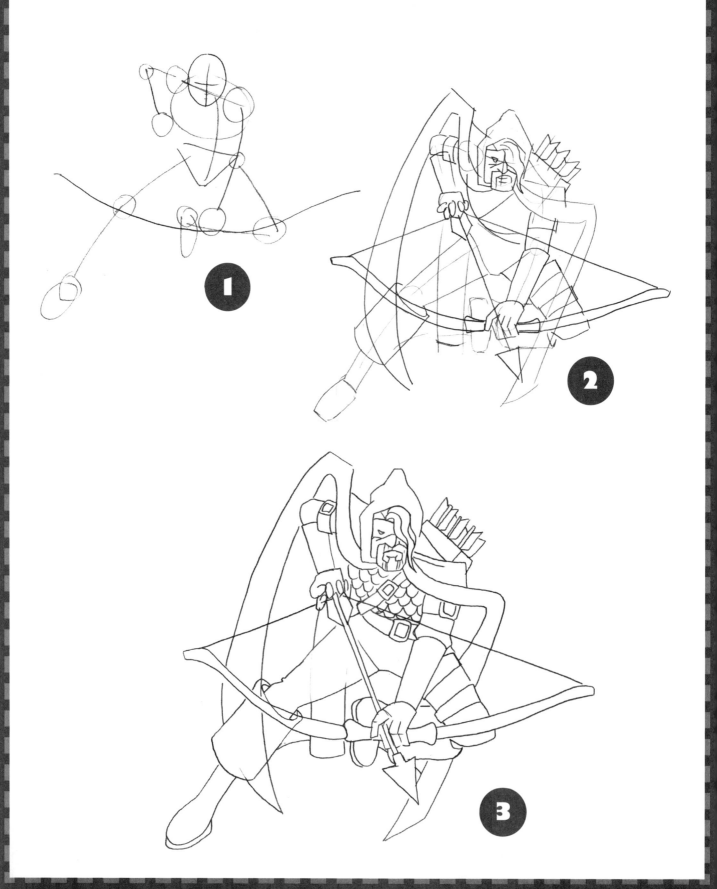

The Hooded Man

ORIGIN: He took over the "Robin Hood" identity from his father.
POWERS: Magic bow and arrows. Super strength.

The Tough Villain

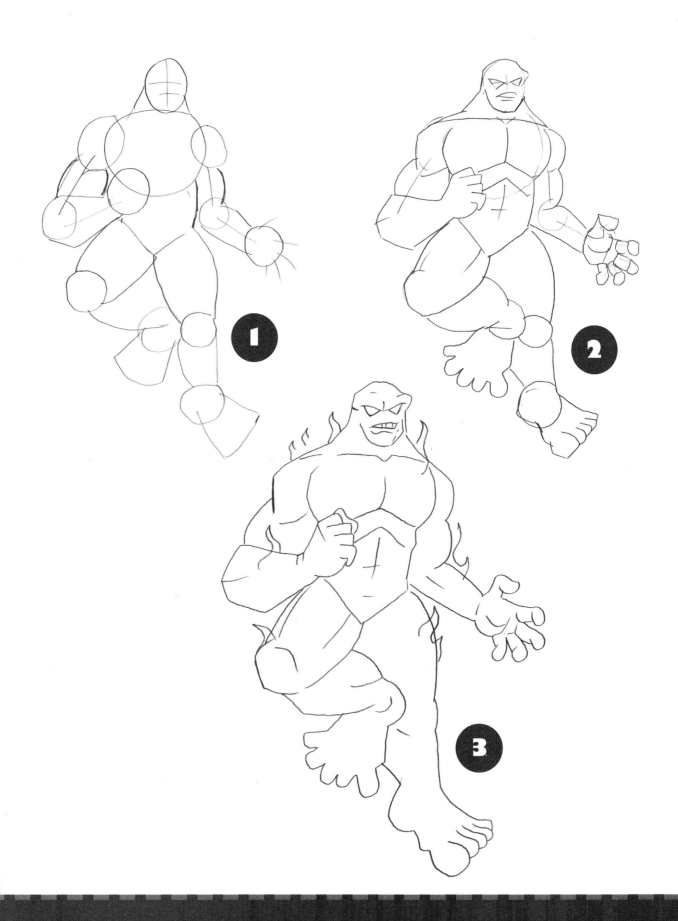

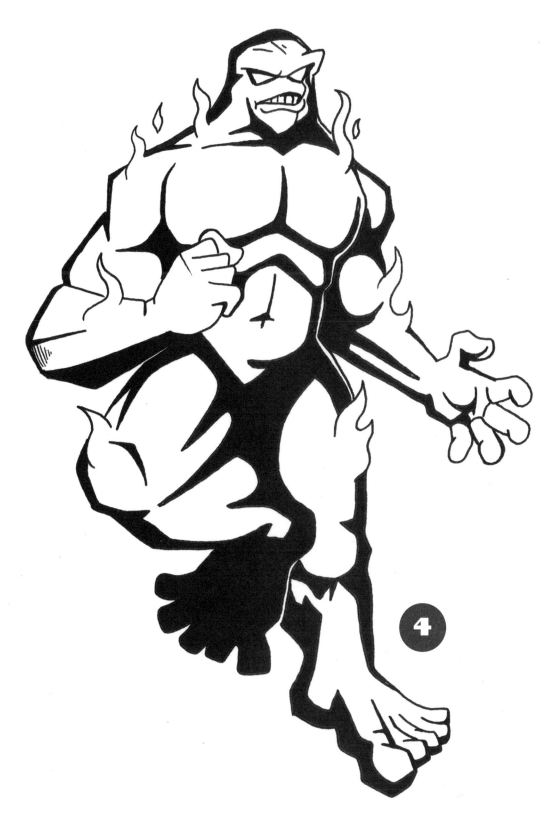

Magma Menace

ORIGIN: Geologist studying lava flows breathed gasses that gave him mutant powers and turned him into a monster.

POWERS: Burns anything he touches. Can turn into lava to squeeze between cracks.

Elemental Creature

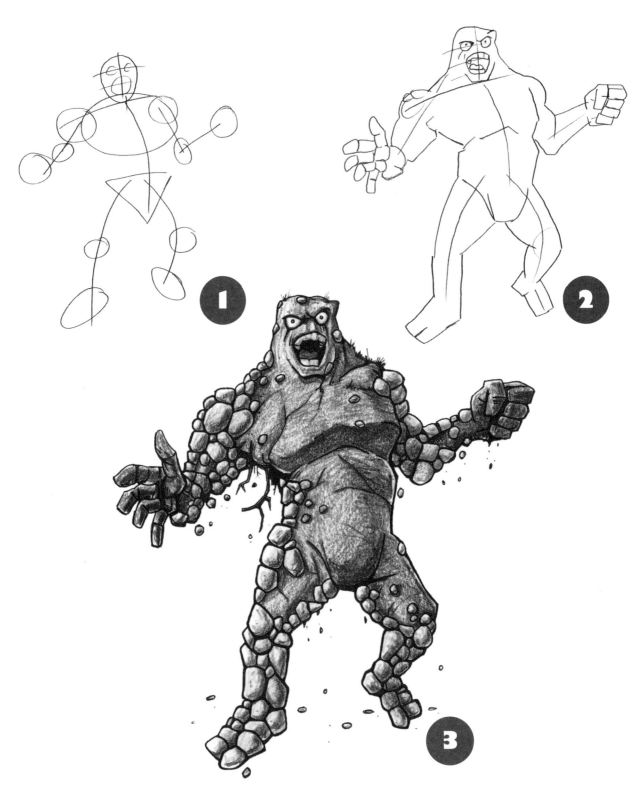

The Groundskeeper

ORIGIN: An elemental creature who has joined humans to fight evil.
POWERS: Superstrong and melts into the earth to travel anywhere on the globe.

Speedster

Hype

ORIGIN: Trained with a government team of teen heroes.
POWERS: Super speed and reflexes.

Thugs

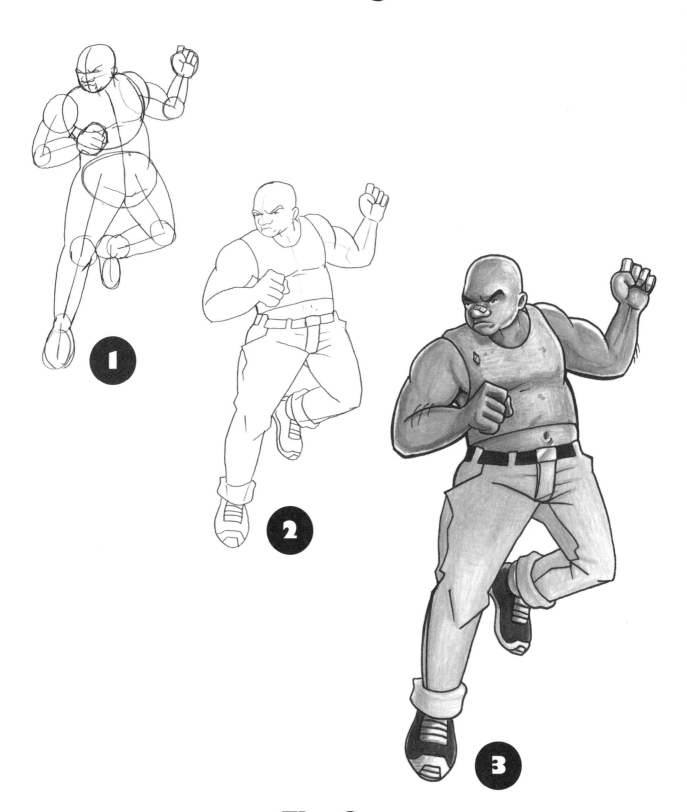

The Goon

ORIGIN: Unknown.

POWERS: No super powers. Has a fair amount of strength, but is not very smart.

The Skullion

ORIGIN: Possessed by Sir Skull, skullions do his dirty work because he is an evil spirit and cannot do it himself.

POWERS: Because they are possesed, they are fearless in battle.

Acrobats

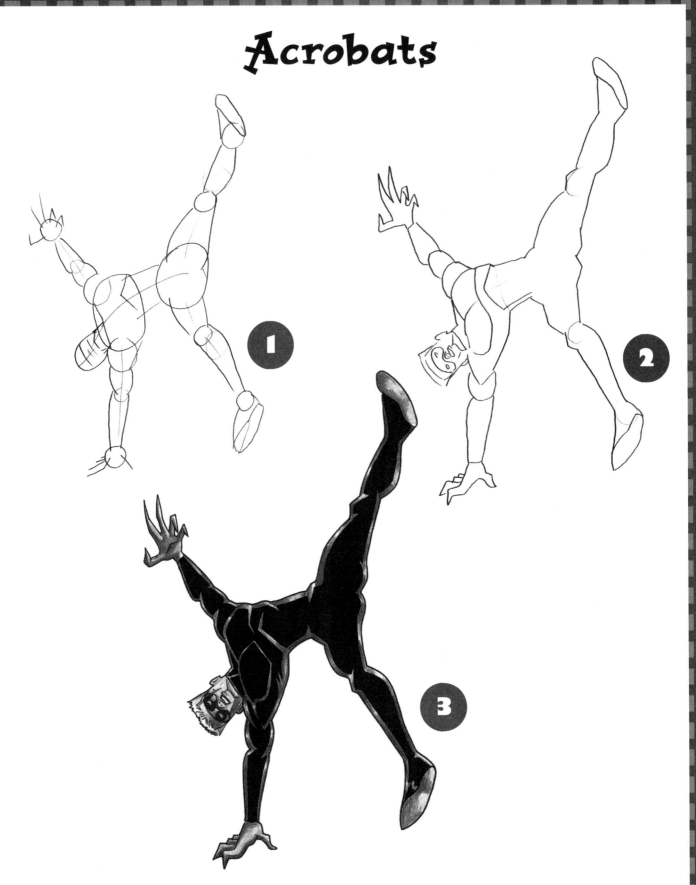

Panther

ORIGIN: A villain who always gets away from police, his origins are still a mystery.
POWERS: Super fast with razor-sharp claws.

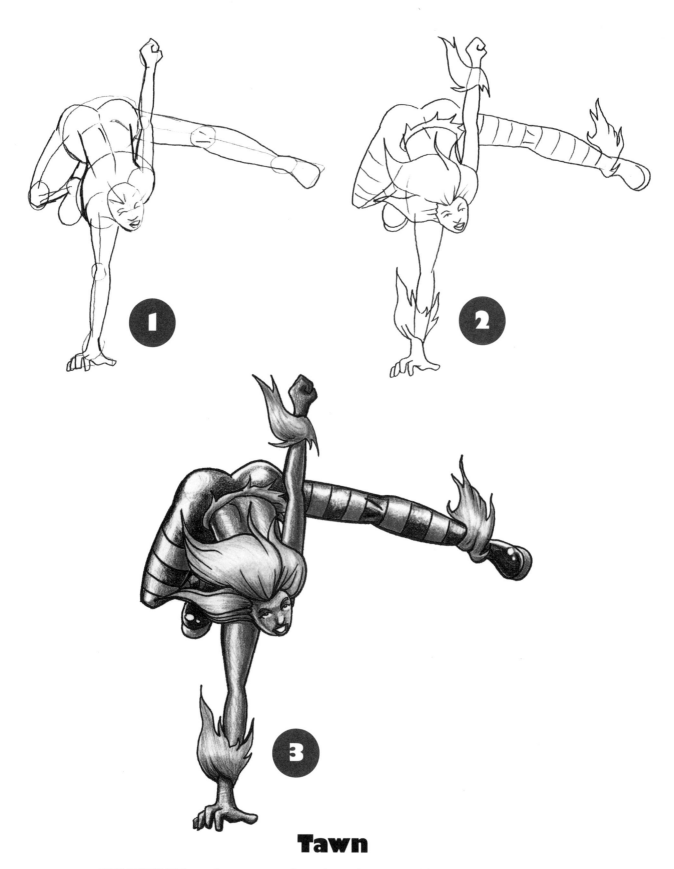

Tawn

ORIGINS: Was a famous cat burglar who turned in her fellow robbers.
POWERS: No super powers. She is a great acrobat and martial artist who is always moving and twisting.

Martial Artists

Tatsu

ORIGIN: A Buddhist monk trained in kung fu who ran away to Japan after a run-in with dragon hunters in China.

POWERS: Can turn into a powerful dragon who can attack with blasts of flame and razor-sharp claws.

Agent Feng

ORIGIN: From a secret group of demon hunters, she battles evil in the city.
POWERS: Can ride the winds to run up walls and even appear to fly.
Outside she can make winds that will lift and control a large truck.

Alien Invaders

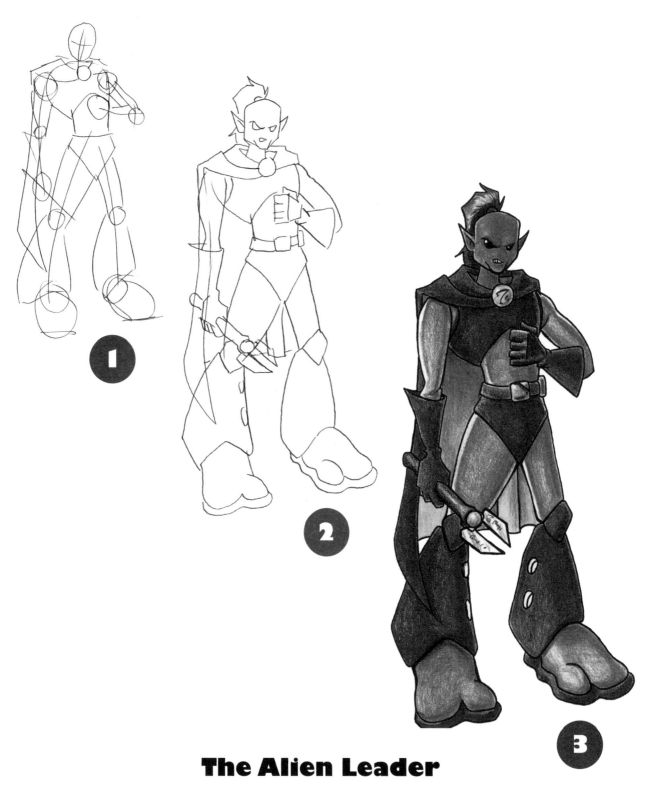

The Alien Leader

ORIGINS: Insect-like and well… alien. It is important to understand why the aliens are invading. Are they just exploring? Do they want power? Know why they are here.
POWERS: Could be any number of things. The leader almost always has many followers to do his fighting for him.

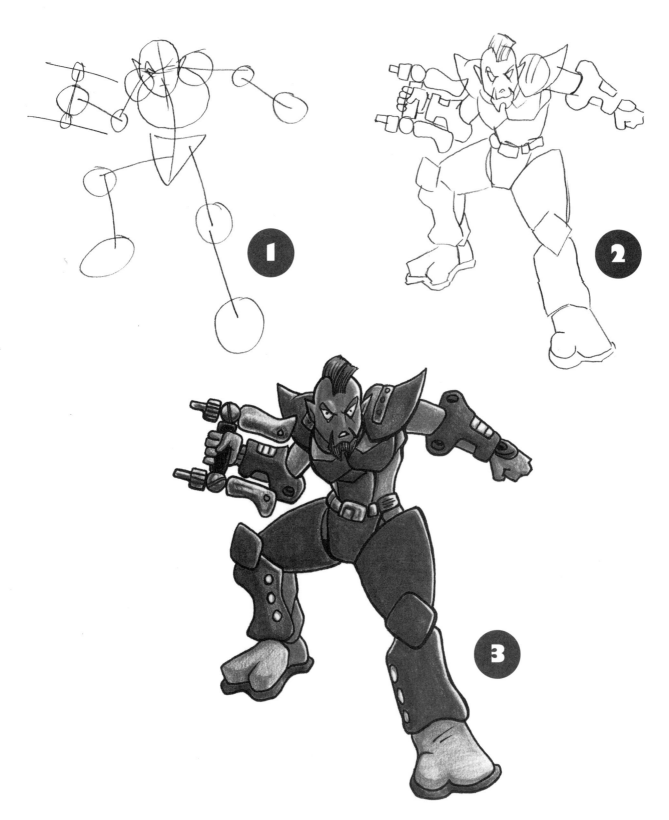

The Alien Fighter

ORIGIN: There only to do the leader's dirty work, they can be nameless, faceless drones or they can be trained fighters.
POWERS: Has alien technology and many alien super-skills.

Monsters

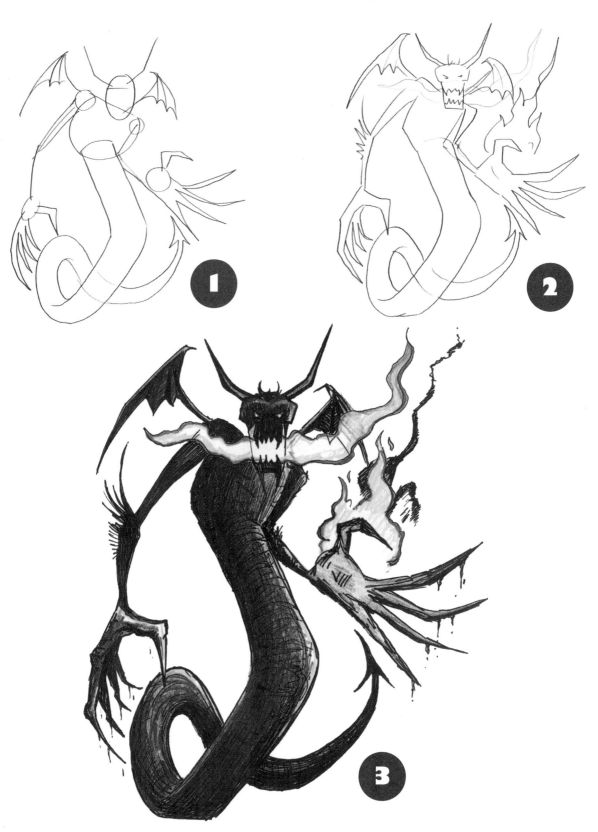

The Demon

Claws, horns and fire—this monster is evil and will be a challenge for even the strongest heroes.

The Vampire

Not all vampires have black capes and pointy teeth. Make them alien, scary and bat-like.

Robots

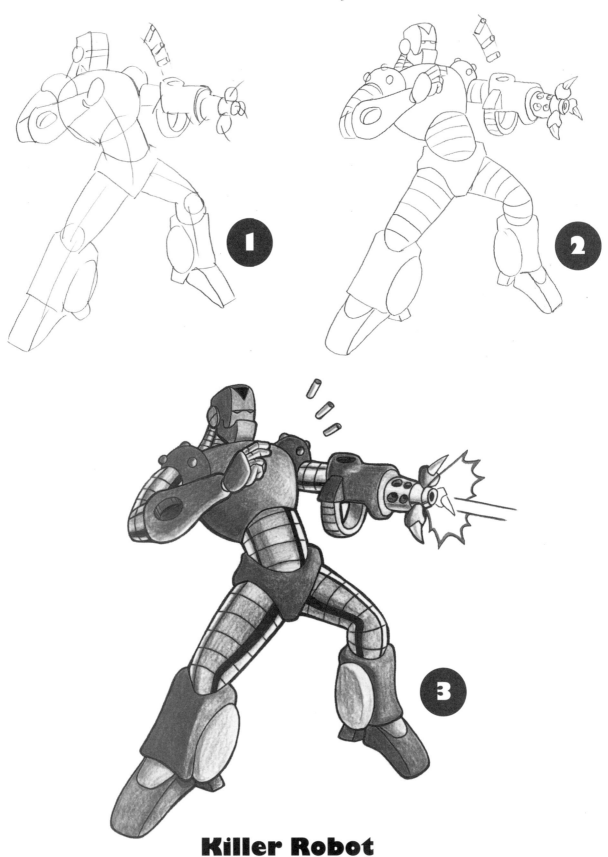

Killer Robot

Unstoppable, this is a destruction machine. It has a laser/machine gun built into its arm.

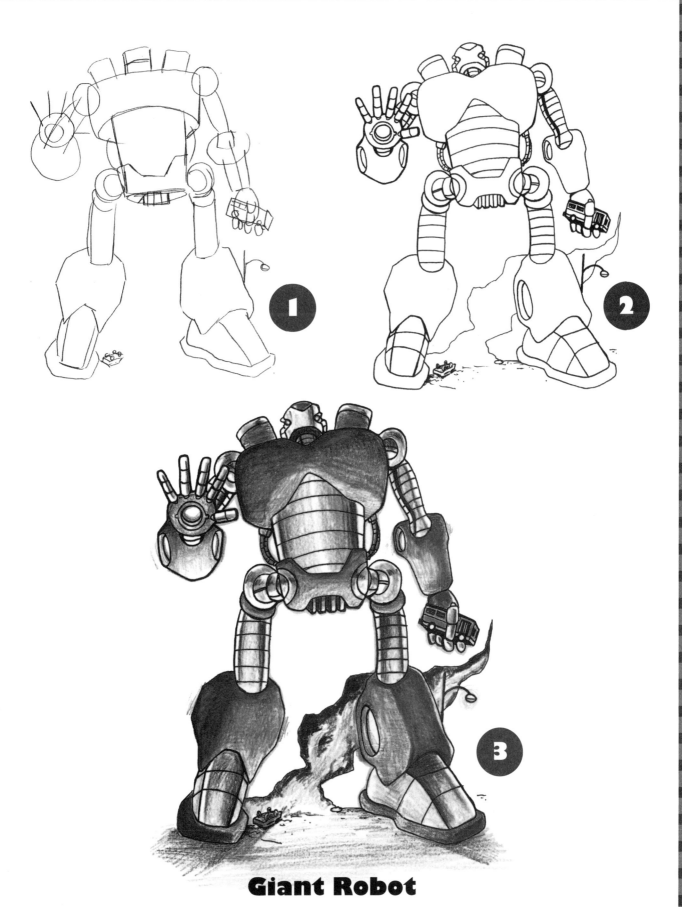

Giant Robot

Giant Robots come from lots of places in comics: alien warriors, military hardware, tools of revenge or broken helpers.

Super Car

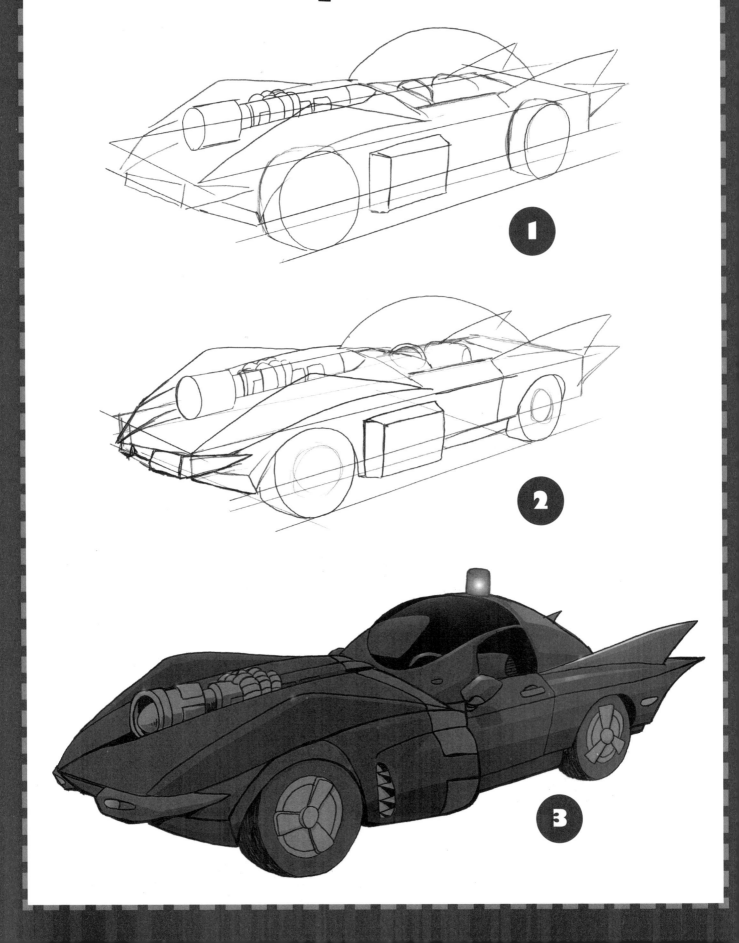

Truck

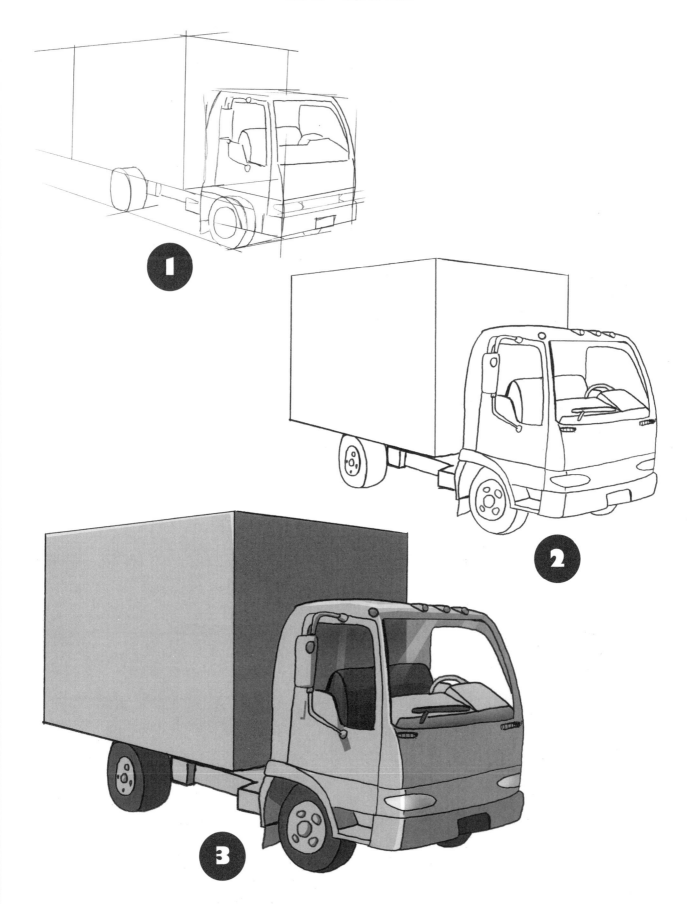

Alien Space Fighter

Alien Space Pod

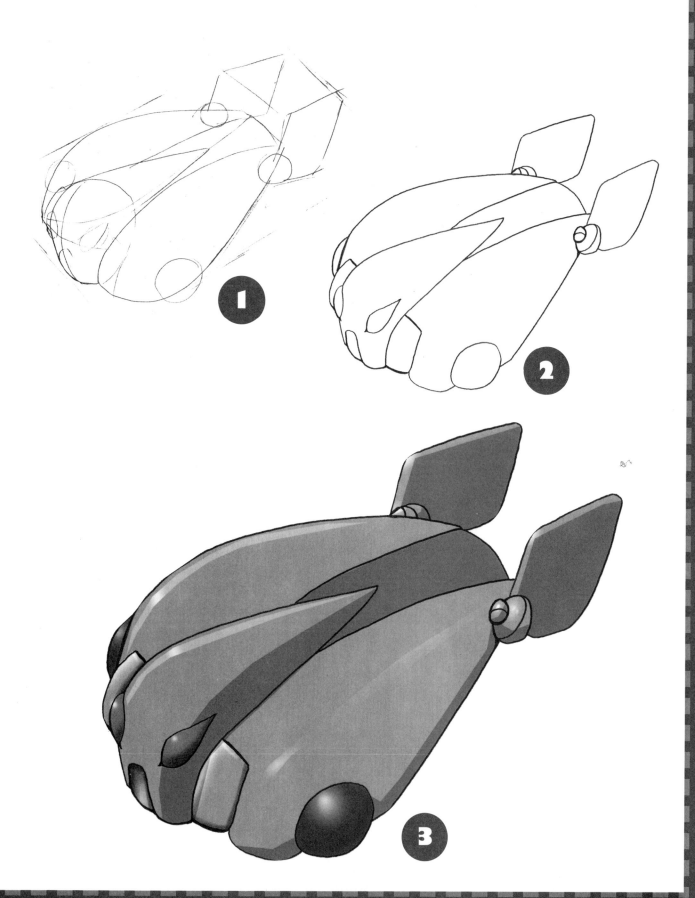

Alien World

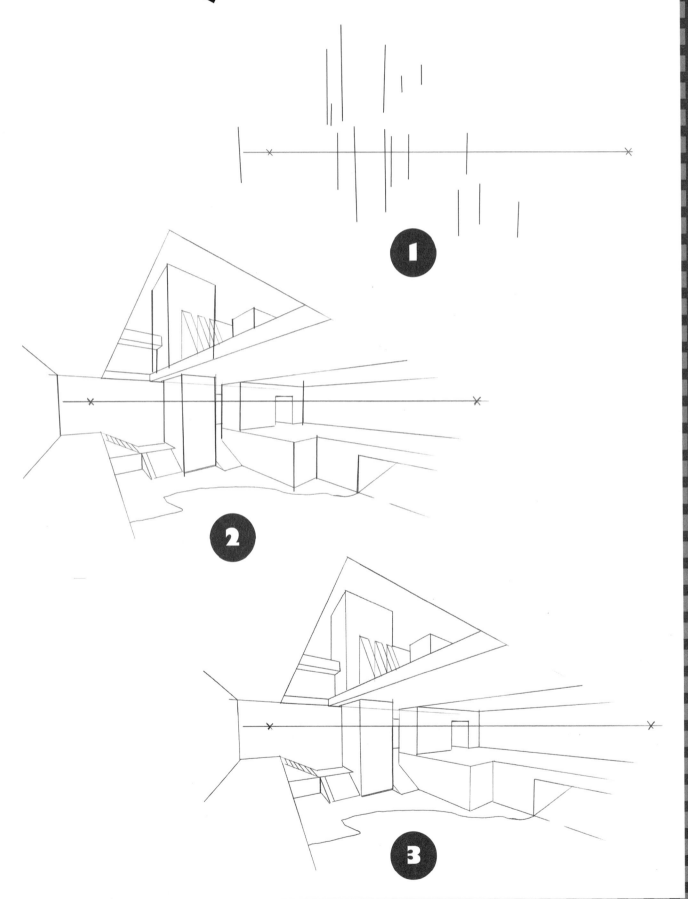

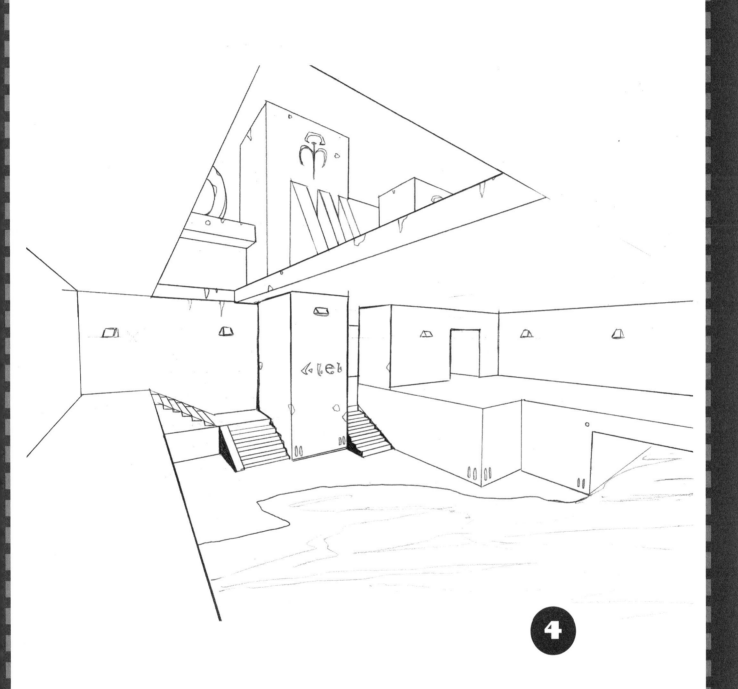

4

City Buildings

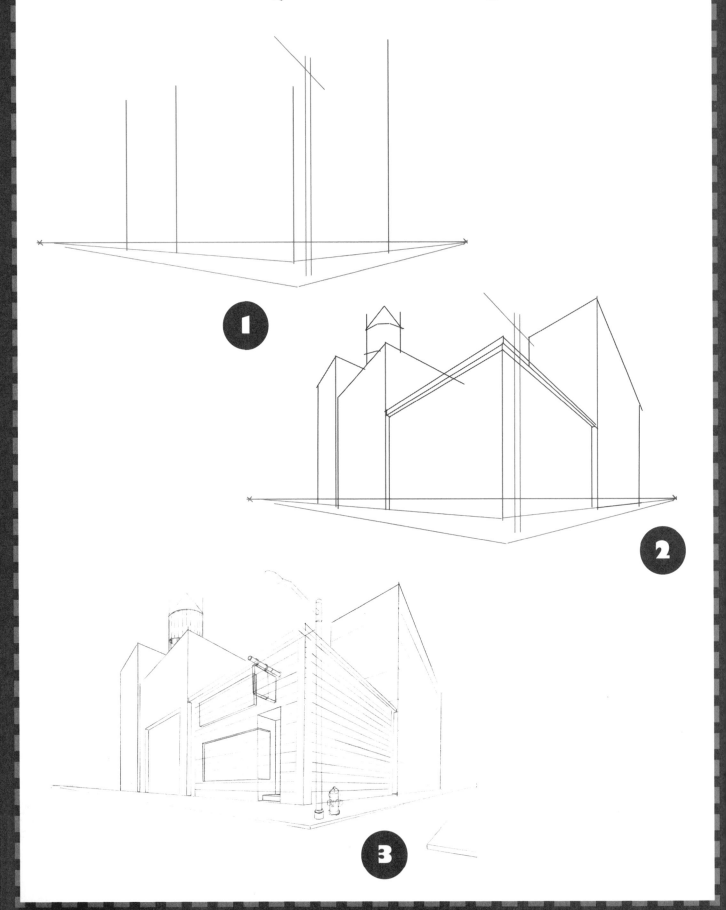

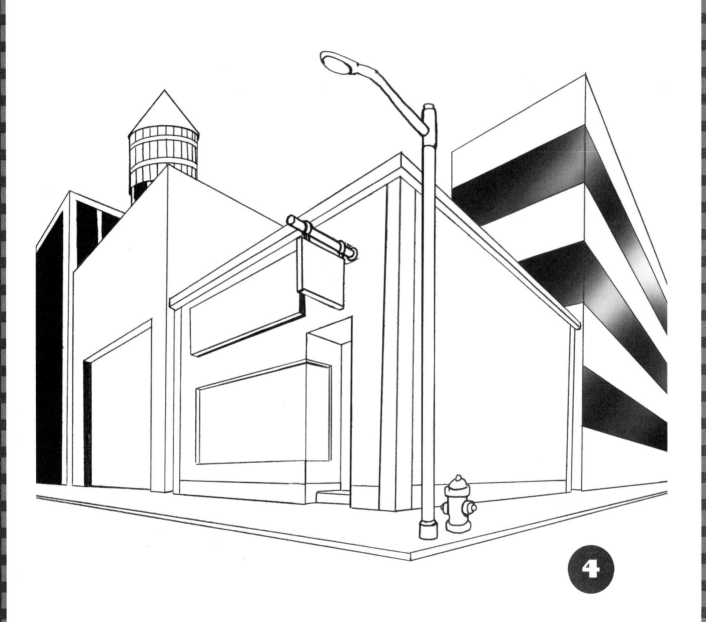

4

Super Technology

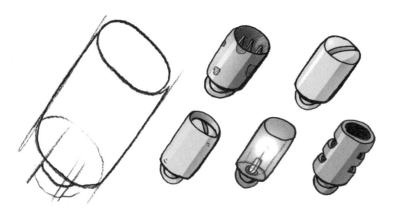

The Bolt

The bolt can be some kind of venting unit, a tightening bolt, a container of cooling fluid or fuel, a lightbulb or some sort of exhaust system. Draw it using basic shapes just like anything else.

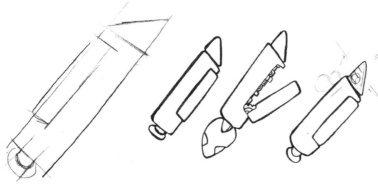

Rabbit Ears

Rabbit ears appear from time to time in comics. The basic shape is a thin rectangle that rises from the surface. They may be sensors, antennae, computer processors or lights.

About the Author

David Okum has worked as a freelance artist and illustrator since 1984 and has had his manga work published since 1992, beginning with a story in a Ninja High School anthology published by Antarctic Press. He has since been included in two other Antarctic Press anthologies and several small-press comic books. His writing and artwork have appeared in six books by Guardians of Order, publishers of Big Eyes, Small Mouth (the anime and manga role-playing game).

David studied fine art and history at the University of Waterloo and works as a high school art teacher.

Other fine Impact books are available from your local bookstore, art supply store or direct from the publisher.

09 08 07 06 05   5 4 3 2 I

DISTRIBUTED IN CANADA BY FRASER DIRECT
100 Armstrong Avenue
Georgetown, ON, Canada L7G 5S4
Tel: (905) 877-4411

DISTRIBUTED IN THE U.K. AND EUROPE BY DAVID & CHARLES
Brunel House, Newton Abbot, Devon, TQ12 4PU, England
Tel: (+44) 1626 323200, Fax: (+44) 1626 323319
Email: mail@davidandcharles.co.uk

DISTRIBUTED IN AUSTRALIA BY CAPRICORN LINK
P.O. Box 704, S. Windsor NSW, 2756 Australia
Tel: (02) 4577-3555

Library of Congress Cataloging in Publication Data

Okum, David, 1967-
    Draw super heroes! / David Okum. — Ist ed.
        p. cm
    ISBN 1-58180-731-7 (pbk. : alk. paper)
    1. Heroes in art--Juvenile literature. 2. Cartooning--Technique--Juvenile literature. I. Title.

NC1764. 8 . H47038 2005
741.5—dc22   2005006211

Editor: Mona Michael
Production editor: Jenny Ziegler
Designer: Wendy Dunning
Production artist: Brian Schroeder
Production coordinator: Mark Griffin

Credit Where Credit's Due

The following people were integral in the creation or inspiration of some of the characters that appear in this book.

Mitch Krajewski: Panther
Caitlin Okum: Gargirl
Jennifer Okum: Windburn
Stephanie Okum: Starlighter
Nick Rintche: Hype and Tatsu

Collect Them All!

These books and other **IMPACT** titles are available at your local arts & craft retailer, bookstore, online supplier or by calling 1-800-448-0915 in North America or 0870 2200220 in the United Kingdom. Visit www.impact-books.com.